CHICHEN ITZA

TEXT
Archeologist Luis A. Martos

COVER
Temple of the Warriors:
the Columns and the Chac Mool

HALF TITLE
Relief on a Ball Court Bench

PHOTOGRAPHS
G. Dagli Orti
M. Calderwood p.14
Monclem Archives

CONACULTA · INAH ❀
Reproduction authorized by the National
Institute of Archaeology and History

© 2008, Monclem Ediciones S.A. de C.V.
Leibnitz 31, colonia Anzures 11590
México, D.F.
www.monclem.com
e-mail: monclem@monclem.com
Tels.: 55 45 07 39 • 52 55 42 48
ISBN 978-970-9019-49-0

Printed by
Stellar Group, S.A. de C.V.
E. Rébsamen 314 y 315, Narvarte
03020, México, D.F.
5639-2342 / 563-1850
September, 2010

Index

Maya Culture

▶ Temple 2 and the North Acropolis at Tikal are typical examples of Maya monumental architecture, which can be recognized by large bases, massive buildings and high cresting decorated with sculptures in stucco. Numerous stelae were raised in the plazas with inscriptions exalting the dynastic history.

The Maya are one of the Americas' most original and complex cultures, which achieved enormous progress in the fields of science and the arts. In antiquity they spread over a vast region of almost 400,000 km^2, which covers the present-day Mexican states of Campeche, Yucatán and Quintana Roo, part of Tabasco and Chiapas, as well as Belize and part of Guatemala, Honduras and the western portion of El Salvador.

Very roughly, Maya territory is divided into three major areas: the Highlands of the South, which include the mountainous areas of Chiapas and Guatemala; the Central Maya Area, which includes the Department of Petén in Guatemala and the adjacent outer valleys; and the Lowlands of the North, which cover the Yucatán Peninsula.

The origin of the Maya goes back to 2500 B.C., when a proto-Maya group established themselves in the Cuchumatan Highlands in the current Department of Huehuetenango in Guatemala. Over time, this group broke up into several Maya-type languages which, owing to different migratory flows, became distributed over the extensive Maya territory.

Although as of 550 B.C. Maya culture began to take shape, it was around 250-300 A.D. that it could be clearly distinguished, free of all outside influence.

During the Early Classic period, between 300 and 600 A.D., a number of cities emerged which grew and developed vigorously, although their maximum splendor was reached during the Late Classic, between 600 and 800 A.D., a time when the most

4

important cities flourished: Tikal, Uaxactún, Copán, Cobá, Calakmul, Toniná, Palenque, Comalcalco, Yaxchilán, Edzná and Becán. At the end of the period, from 800 to 900 A.D., the "Maya collapse" took place, a phenomenon possibly explained by a serious sociopolitical crisis; this is evident because the construction of buildings and the erection of stelae ceased, production and exchange of polychrome ceramics was interrupted and most of the Maya cities were abandoned. Although the causes of the collapse are not accurately known, it is possible to attribute it to the conjunction of several factors, among them a prolonged drought of more than 80 years, soil depletion, growth of the bureaucratic apparatus, sociopolitical problems and the inrush of migrant groups.

As of 987 A.D. and up to 1200 A.D. the Maya tradition of the north of Yucatán fused with Toltec culture from Central Mexico. This superimposition of traditions gave rise the Maya-Toltec culture, which established its capital in Chichén Itzá and is representative of the Early Post-Classic in Yucatán.

The city was destroyed around 1250 A.D. by the *Cocom*, who

exercised a centralized power from their capital, Mayapán. Later, in about 1441 A.D., the *Tutul Xiu* razed Mayapán and established the new capital in Maní. As of that time the Yucatán Peninsula became organized into 16 independent domains, and remained so until the arrival of the Spaniards in the 16th century.

The Maya defined their own artistic style which they expressed in architecture, sculpture, stucco modeling, mural painting, stonework and polychrome ceramics; both the execution of the works and the themes are very uniform.

They also built large, perfectly planned urban centers with spectacular architecture, which stand out for their high temple-pyramids, palaces, sanctuaries, ball courts and major building complexes with multiple rooms and patios raised on platforms of various levels, the so-called acropolises. A significant Maya feature is the incorporation of sculpture into the architecture, as can be seen in the façades, crests and bodies of the pyramids, where there are almost always large masks and stucco reliefs.

Maya architecture is also well known for the use of the "false arch" or "Maya vault", an element used to roof rooms and accesses, and the famous "arches", votive monuments built at the beginning of the *sacbeoob* (paths that interconnected the different architectural complexes and also one city with others).

The social structure was pyramidal, headed by the sovereign known as *Halach Uinic* (True Man), the representative of a heredi-

▼ The Maya developed a complex system of logosyllabic writing made up of almost 850 characters, some phonetic and others logographic (which express ideas).

tary dynasty. Under him were the nobles, the priests, the warriors, the traders and the artisans; at the base of the pyramid were the peasants and then the slaves.

The economic base was agriculture and the Maya therefore developed intensive cultivation systems, such as hill terraces, raised fields in low-lying lands and pipe and irrigation systems in river and lake areas. The basic crops were corn, chili, squash, cotton and cacao.

Trade was also very important since it favored exchanges of diverse objects such as ceramics, textiles, jade, conch, flint, obsidian, skins, honey, salt and other products both locally and regionally.

One of the major achievements of Maya culture was the development of a system of hieroglyphic writing, fully constituted at least by the year 250 B.C. and considered a sacred means of communication. For that reason, the *Aj dzib* or scribe used to be a noble of the reigning dynasty.

The inscriptions were carved on stone, stelae, lintels, panels and stairways, on stucco reliefs, mural painting, ceramics, codices and even on jade and bone. The writing system was "logosyllabic", that is, some signs symbolized syllabic sounds and others ideas or actions. The topics of the texts are essentially historical and religious; they narrate the way of life and activities of the nobility, deeds of the lords and the gods, alliances, weddings to unite lineages, births of future lords, death of important dignitaries, rise to power, wars, capture and sacrifice of some lord, construction and consecration of temples, holding of ceremonies, etc.

The numbering system was vigesimal, based on the position of the values and the use of zero, which was a conch-shaped design. The dot indicated units and the bar had a value of five; there were also ideograms to represent the numbers from zero to 19.

The Maya had two calendars: a sacred one or *Tzolkin* of 260 days and a civil one or *Haab* of 365 days made up of 18 months of 20 days, plus five ill-omened days known as the *Uayeb* days. They also calculated very accurately the movements of the sun and moon and the cycles of Venus, and predicted eclipses.

The Maya had a complicated vision of the cosmos and a polytheistic religion in which god the creator was Itzamná; *Chaac* was the god of rain; the sun god had various names: *Ah Kin, Kinich Ahau* or *Kinich Kakmo*; the goddess of the moon, medicine and childbirth was *Ix Chel*, who had an oracle on the island of Cozumel; the god of trade was *Ek Chuah* and that of death *Ah Puch*. Toward the 10th century the plumed serpent *Kukulkán* was incorporated into the Maya pantheon, undoubtedly an influence from Central Mexico.

Chichén Itzá through time

▶ Lithograph by Frederick Catherwood of the Castle
at Chichén Itzá; this English draughtsman and the
explorer John L. Stephens visited the site in 1840.

For more than nine centuries Chichén Itzá was one of the most important cities in northern Yucatán. It had long periods of construction activity and reached its greatest monumentality between 800 and 1100 A.D. During this period it became the most important and sumptuous political and religious center in the area. Recent archaeological work has proven that its occupation goes back at least to 150 B.C., although its first flowering took place around 550 A.D., reaching its maximum splendor around 987 A.D., when it became the capital of the legendary Itzaes, a group that developed the monumental Maya-Toltec style.

During its era of greatest growth, the city covered an area of 25 km² and its population exceeded 30,000 inhabitants. The natural setting was very important for the choice of settlement, since the area is rich in fertile lands suitable for agriculture and fresh-water cenotes abound. Undoubtedly the sacred cenote, with its renowned and age-old cult, represented an important ritual and symbolic factor that was decisive to the founding of the city. In fact, most of the main residential groups of the ancient city are distributed around one of these water circles, as occurs with the Grupo del Osario which was built next to the Xtoloc cenote. Also important was the presence of caves, "sascaberas" and "rejolladas"; the former were used as mines to obtain stone and *sascab* powder for construction; the latter, which were natural depressions, served for intensive agriculture.

The axis of the site is a great central complex, the political, religious and administrative heart of the ancient city, made up of a vast plaza with El Castillo at the center. Around this nucleus are 20 ceremonial and residential complexes and innumerable smaller complexes, all joined by a complicated network of 75 *sacbeoob* or white paths. However, in the internal layout of the site one can recognize the city's two architectural components, vestiges of this civilization's two most important epochs.

Around 700 A.D. Chichén Itzá became consolidated as an important settlement and political center. It is possible that the city was called at that time *Uuc-yab-nal*, a phrase that could be translated as "the seven rich ears of corn," and was made up of several archi-

8

tectural complexes, among them the House of the Deer, the Red Temple or Chichanchob, the Akab Dzib, the substructure of the Red Jaguar of the Castle and the Complex of the Nuns, the latter perhaps the most important one. During those years the city was dominated by *Puuc* style architecture, made up of large buildings with numerous rooms, whose façades were decorated with mosaics at the base and ornamental friezes with lattice-work, large masks of the god of rain and geometrical features in the upper part.

As of 900 A.D., with the arrival of the *Itzaes*, the city underwent a transformation and acquired a new appearance under the style known as Maya-Toltec. The architecture was now distinguished by vast roofed spaces with vaults supported by colonnades, the use of columns with capitals similar to rattlesnakes, stairways delimited by struts finished off with snakes, use of atlas-like sculptures, *Chac Mool* sculptures, friezes decorated with processions of jaguars, eagles and coyotes, etc. In this new Chichén Itzá, the spaces and buildings had a concentric distribution within a disperse settlement, with a network of paths as features of integration; apparently, the typical architectural pattern was that of the temple, altar and patio or patio-gallery.

It was also during this second epoch that the city was rechristened "Chichén Itzá", that is, "in the mouth of the well of the *Itzaes*,

9

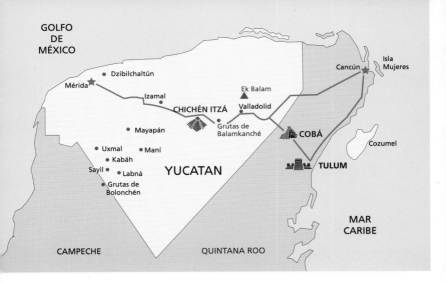

according to the etymological derivatives *chi* (mouth) and *chen* (well). However, it is also possible that Itzá meant "water wizard", so the full translation could be "in the mouth of the well of the water wizards."

Several hypotheses have sought to explain the origin of the *Itzaes*. The most commonly accepted one maintains that it was actually a question of the *Putunes*, a Maya Chontal group from the region of Chontalpa on the Gulf of Mexico. According to the chronicles of the *Chilam Balam*, this group organized two invasions toward Yucatán known as the "big descent," begun in 918 A.D. and the "small descent," around 987 A.D. The first extended through much of the east and south of the Yucatán Peninsula and the second through the north. It has been suggested that the big descent resulted from dominion and control of a trade route that went inland through the Southern Lowlands; these events could have favored, directly or indirectly, the collapse of the Classic period. Prior to the little descent, the *Itzaes* may have tried to usurp that route, the consequence of which was the reorganization of new trade networks toward the north of the peninsula, both overland and maritime.

Whatever the explanation, the fact is that around the 8th century the *Itzaes* invaded the Caribbean region. First they occupied the island of Cozumel, then moved onto terra firma and penetrated the peninsula through the coastal location of Polé (today Xcaret). From there they advanced toward the interior of the peninsula through different provinces, until they settled definitively in Chichén Itzá, around the year 918 A.D. The *Itzaes* likely controlled Cozumel due to its religious and commercial importance, and also the region of Ascensión and Espíritu Santo Bays, where they established commercial ports.

Toward 1200 A.D. Chichén Itzá came to its end, and the causes that precipitated its extinction are still not known with certainty. The chronicles mention a dispute with Mayapán and an intrigue with a lord known as *Hunac Ceel Cauich*. In any event, the *Itzaes* were defeated and the city was abandoned The group emigrated to the south up to Lake Petén Itzá in Guatemala, where they founded a new city, Tayasal, which remained until well into the 17th century and was the last Maya redoubt to surrender to Spanish dominion.

The oldest and most complete description of the city is that of Fray Diego de Landa in the 16th century, but it was John L. Stephens and draughtsman Frederick Catherwood who brought the existence of Chichén Itzá to the world after publishing their book "Incidents of Travel in Yucatán" in 1843.

Throughout the 19th century a number of travelers and explorers visited the site and left testimony of their impressions. Such are the cases of B. M. Norman, Baron Frederichstahl, Augustus Le Plongeon, Alfred P. Maudslay, Desiré Charnay, William Holmes and Teobert Maler. In 1894, Edward Thompson bought the Hacienda of Chichén Itzá and devoted himself to studying the site, although not in a very scientific manner since, for example, he dredged the cenote.

▼ The Castle during the spring equinox, when the sun projects on the side of the beam a serpent of light and one of shade that represent the descent of *Kukulkán*, the plumed serpent.

Map of Chichén Itzá

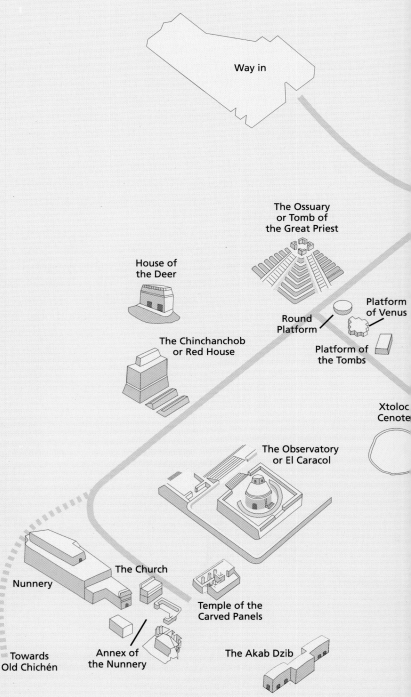

Way in

The Ossuary
or Tomb of
the Great Priest

House of
the Deer

Round
Platform

Platform
of Venus

Platform of
the Tombs

The Chinchanchob
or Red House

Xtoloc
Cenote

The Observatory
or El Caracol

The Church

Nunnery

Temple of the
Carved Panels

Towards
Old Chichén

Annex of
the Nunnery

The Akab Dzib

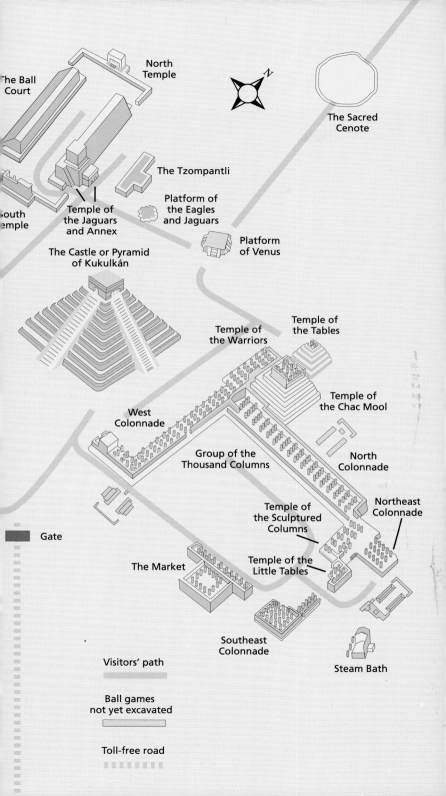

The Ball Court

North Temple

N

The Sacred Cenote

The Tzompantli

South Temple

Temple of the Jaguars and Annex

Platform of the Eagles and Jaguars

Platform of Venus

The Castle or Pyramid of Kukulkán

Temple of the Warriors

Temple of the Tables

Temple of the Chac Mool

West Colonnade

Group of the Thousand Columns

North Colonnade

Temple of the Sculptured Columns

Northeast Colonnade

Gate

The Market

Temple of the Little Tables

Southeast Colonnade

Steam Bath

Visitors' path

Ball games not yet excavated

Toll-free road

Monuments and Art
in Chichén Itzá

▼ The Castle, the Temple of the Warriors and the Thousand Columns are the main buildings of the Maya-Toltec period. They were at the heart of the ancient city, the political, religious and administrative center.

Temple of the Jaguars

The Temple of the Jaguars backs onto the far south end of the eastern platform of the Ball Court. It is a large base on which a magnificent building of two vaulted galleries rises. Outstanding is the access portico with two impressive columns whose bases take the form of serpents' heads and the capitals of rattlesnakes. The frieze, delimited by moldings of intertwined serpents, is decorated with reliefs sculptured with stone mosaics; outstanding is a procession of jaguars marching through *chimallis* or shields typical of Central Mexico. The roof is finished with battlements in the form of shields crossed by arrows. The interior of the temple was profusely decorated with murals of which some vestiges remain; the scene of a battle waged in front of a village with palm huts is worthy of note. The lintel of access to the interior is a richly carved piece of zapote wood.

▼The rings of the ball game, decorated with intertwined feathered serpents, marked the center of the court. It has been suggested that in the fortuitous event that the ball passed through one of the rings, the game ended and the team that had succeeded in doing so was the winner.

16

The Ball Court

With a length of 168 m and 70 m wide, Chichén Itzá's ball court is not only the largest in the Maya world, but also in the whole of ancient Mexico. The court is completely closed in and its ground plan takes the form of the letter "I"; it is flanked to the east and west by two platforms 95 m long whose vertical walls are 8 m high and it has low banked footways. At the very center of the walls are the stone rings that mark the middle of the court and they are decorated with reliefs of intertwined plumed serpents. On the outside, the platforms display broad staircases delimited by beams which allowed access to the upper terrace, where there were three small square rooms, which perhaps were used as temples or areas for the lords, nobles or priests.

The Ball Court, built during the Maya-Toltec period, had important religious and astronomic significance: the court represents the cosmos and men are the divine forces that move the stars, symbolized by the ball. The object of the game was not to pass the ball through the rings but to move it from one side to the other without it being stopped, like stars that cannot stop.

Reliefs of the Slopes

The slopes of the footways have panels decorated in elaborate bas-reliefs showing processions of ball player-warriors, seven on each side of a prominent circular central motif displaying the figure of a ball with an inscribed human skull, symbol of death. All the personages, which could represent two teams of seven players, are richly decked out with helmets of zoomorphic figures and fine feather headdresses and ear and bar nose guards; they also wear short skirts, conch-shaped breastplates, arm protection disks, wide yoke-like belts with palms at the front, knee guards, insignias and ornaments.

The best preserved relief is that of the eastern slope, in which the central scene with the representation of a decapitation sacrifice can be distinguished: the player on the right, with one knee guard on the ground, has been decapitated and from his neck spouts copious blood in the form of six serpents; a plant with flowers comes out of the jaws of one of them. Standing to the left of the victim is the executioner brandishing a knife in one hand while the other holds the head of the decapitated man by the hair.

Temple of the South

The Temple of the South is a building that had an ample vaulted space and stands out due to the great portico of seven access openings. Each of the pilasters of the portico is decorated with a different relief; warriors are represented there with hieroglyphs indicating their name, perhaps the members of a clan or lineage, whereas at the base the figure of *Kukulkán* appears.

Temple of the North

To the north and to the south, the ball court is closed off by various buildings. The one to the north, also known as "Temple of the Bearded Man" for the representation of a man with a beard, is a construction of one single vaulted room, with an ample access portico with two columns. The vault is profusely decorated with reliefs framed in red; there are four main scenes involving more than forty people dressed in rich attire very similar to those of the procession of warriors of the court's footways: in the upper part, four individuals preside over a ritual of the famous phallic cult; below, on the next level, there is a decapitation ceremony; in the remaining two scenes a number of warriors, temples and trees can be identified. The building stands on a low base in three sections, with a staircase toward the south, delimited by beams decorated with reliefs of trees supported by the monster of the earth and covered by climbing plants and flowers over which birds and butterflies flutter and alight. Over the trees the image of *Kukulkán* appears, represented as a man emerging from the jaws of a feathered serpent.

Annex of the Temple of the Jaguars

This building is located at the level of the plaza, next to the back façade, that is, the one on the eastern side of the Temple of the Jaguars. It is a small edifice with a single vaulted chamber and a portico made up of two pilasters decorated with reliefs. In the central opening of the access there is a beautiful throne in the form of a jaguar, symbol of power and royalty among the ancient Maya.

Both the walls and the vault are covered with bas-reliefs with scenes of processions of warriors headed by "Captain Solar Disk," who looks to the front toward "Captain Serpent," who in turn is looking upwards. "Captain Solar Disk," also known as *Kakupakal*, appears in the upper part of the image, that is, on a privileged and celestial plane related to dead predecessors, *Kukulkán* and the sun. Both lords seem to be guiding several groups of warriors who carry slings and are wearing butterfly breastplates and elaborate headdresses. The rest of the composition includes scrolls, hooks, braids and plant elements.

The access pilasters also show beautiful reliefs with representations of warriors decked out with showy helmets of birds and feathers, ear guards, breastplates, bracelets, emblems and lances with feathers. The composition also includes *Kukulkán* in his role as lord of the earth and vegetation.

The Tzompantli

In Náhuatl *Tzompantli* means "row of skulls" and it is undoubtedly an element that comes from Central Mexico. It was a votive building, erected to exalt death as the passage to a new life. It is likely that on this construction palings were raised in which the skulls of captured and decapitated warriors were threaded through the temples.

The Tzompantli is situated to the east of the ball court; it is a long platform 60 m long by 12 m wide, with a central projection that gives it a ground plan in the form of a "T". Its walls have a small slope in the lower part and a panel adorned with three rows of reliefs with human skulls outlined in profile. In the central projection of the platform we can recognize representations of eagles and warriors holding human heads in their hands. In 1875, Le Plongeon carried out some excavations there and unearthed a *Chac Mool*.

▲Platform of the Eagles and the Jaguars

The Platform of the Eagles is a small square base with steps on all four sides; the beams look like bodies of plumed serpents whose heads emerge from the tops shaped like dice. The walls have low slopes and boards decorated with panels showing eagles and jaguars devouring human hearts. In the cornice is *Kukulkán* appearing as a reclining warrior wearing eye patches and brandishing a lance. Perhaps the motifs allude to Venus and the daytime and nighttime sun and, therefore, to the cycles of light and dark, life, death and rebirth. The reliefs are very similar to those of the *coatepantli* of Tula, Hidalgo in Central Mexico

▶ Representation of the man-bird-serpent symbolizing *Kukulkán*.

◀ A jaguar, symbol of the night sun, devours a heart in a panel of the Platform of the Eagles and Jaguars.

▼ Platform of Venus

It lies to the north of the Castle and is similar to the Platform of the Eagles, although with larger dimensions and different iconography. The panels show reliefs of a bundle joined to a half flower as a symbol of Venus; the braided mat or "pop", related to power and the throne, also appears. In the panels we recognize the effigy of *Kukulkán*, represented as a man emerging from the jaws of a plumed serpent with eagle's claws. The motifs evoke the deity as the lord of the year, power and rebirth. In the 19th century the sculpture of a *Chac Mool* was discovered inside the structure.

The Castle or Temple of Kukulkán

Is a magnificent pyramid 24 m high; it has a square base and is made up of nine sloping parts with rectangular moldings and slightly rounded corners. It has a stairway facing each of the directions, but the northern is the main one and its beams are finished off with enormous serpents' heads, symbols of *Kukulkán*. Each staircase has 91 steps, which add up to 364, a figure undoubtedly linked to the astronomic calendar. Likewise, there are 26 spaces set into the rectangular moldings of each body, that is, a total of 52 per façade, a number related to the Maya century of 52 years. The upper temple is a sober building set on a quadrangular base and has four accesses: three simple ones with a single doorway and the northern one,

24

which is the main one and has a portico with two serpent-shaped pilasters whose bases are the head and the capital the rattles. The interior consists of a vestibule which precedes a vaulted sanctuary held up by two pilasters, whereas the other accesses lead to a narrow gallery which runs behind the sanctuary. Both the jambs and the pillars show beautiful reliefs of warriors clad in rich finery, elaborate headdresses, ornaments and insignias.

The façade consists of a plain surface with a sloping base and a frieze delimited by moldings and decorated with sunken panels; over the portico there is a large mask of the god of rain. The roof is finished off with parapets in the form of cut conch, a symbol of the wind.

▲ The Castle's Stairways

Observation of the heavens enabled the Maya to develop a calendar, a vital element for knowledge of the seasons and natural cycles, which were made to coincide with those of society itself. The stars marked cosmic directions which were references for orienting buildings. The Castle is a good example, since during the spring (March 21-23) and autumn (September 21-23) equinoxes, as of four in the afternoon, the sun projects the shadow of the bodies of the pyramid onto the side of the western beam of the northern façade and creates seven triangles of light that unite with the large stone head that finishes the base with its jaws open. For the Maya, this phenomenon was a solar hierophany: the descent of *Kukulkán* as a serpent of light to initiate the agricultural cycle.

The Temple of the Red Jaguar

During the explorations of El Castillo a very similar substructure was discovered, but of smaller proportions. It is also a pyramid with nine sections and reaches a height of 16 m. The façade of the temple that finishes it has a frieze delimited by triple moldings and is decorated with intertwined serpents and a procession of jaguars that alternate with shields. The interior displays two parallel bays; the front one stands out for the presence of *Chac Mool* with bone incrustations in

the eyes, teeth and nails. The back chamber has a beautiful throne made of stone in the form of a jaguar painted in vivid red, with jade incrustations that look like the spots on the skin and jade eyes and carved bone fangs; the seat is made up of a magnificent disk worked in mosaics of turquoise and conch forming a four-serpent design.

▼ Son et Lumière

During the eight months of the dry season the spectacle of light and sound takes place at night. This combines the illumination of various buildings with music and voices that narrate the history and legends of the ancient city. A full moon or a star-filled sky is usually the backdrop to this great show.

The Sacred Cenote

North of the Castle, next to the Platform of Venus, begins *sacbe 1*, which has a length of 270 m and leads to the Sacred Cenote, whose rough beauty attracted the attention of explorers and travelers over the ages. The first description of this extraordinary well dates back to the 16th century and is owed to Fray Diego de Landa:

"A beautiful wide causeway runs from the patio, in front of these theaters to a well about two stones' throws away. In this well they had the custom at that time of throwing in living men in sacrifices to the gods during the dry season and they thought they did not die although they never saw them again. They also threw many valuable stones that were much prized by them."

The cenote is oval shaped and measures 50 m by 60 m, with a height of 22 m from the edge to the water level and has a depth of 20 m. The bottom is muddy and the water cloudy, since there are algae and microorganisms in suspension that give the water a greenish hue, although the surrounding vegetation is also a factor.

Landa mentioned that at the edge of the cenote there was a temple with numerous idols, jars and life-size sculptures of jaguars and

human beings dressed with real ornaments. In fact, the rocky edge was leveled and conditioned, especially at the southern end, where a small temple with two bays was built. The latter was subsequently modified to house a temazcal or steam bath, used perhaps to purify the victim or the priest.

Between 1904 and 1911, Edward H. Thompson used a dredge to systematically plunder the bottom of the cenote. Thus he extracted a number of objects which he then took out of the country illegally, among them numerous vessels, human bones, objects made of jade, conch, turquoise, obsidian, wood, textiles and the famous gold disks. In 1961, the National Institute of Anthropology and History, in collaboration with the National Geographic, carried out a new exploration coordinated by William Folan. For a long time it was believed that the Maya threw young virgins into the cenote. However, recent studies showed that this belief was erroneous, as 64% of the bone remains were children's and only 36% adults (mainly men). Some rituals related to the cenote cult, in addition to offering of objects, included sacrifices, disembowelments and decapitations.

▲ Disk of jade and turquoise mosaics located in the substructure of The Warriors. Similar objects were thrown into the Sacred Cenote as offerings.

29

◀ Detail of a relief of *Kukulkán* represented as a man emerging from the jaws of a plumed serpent, a very recurrent theme in Chichén Itzá. Façade of the Temple of the Warriors.

Temple of the Warriors

The Temple of the Warriors, together with the structure of a Thousand Columns, closes the great plaza on the eastern side. This square-based building has four stepped sections and friezes decorated with jaguars, eagles and a mythical animal, all in the act of devouring hearts. We can also recognize reclining gods with eye patches and lances, perhaps as representations of Venus under the guise of the *Tlachitonatiuh*, that is, the rising sun after its journey through the underworld.

The struts of the stairways show reliefs of plumed serpents which finish off in an upper dado from which the heads emerge and on which sculptures of standard-bearers are also erected.

The upper temple is a square building with an access portico in three sections separated by columns that adopt the form of one-eyed snakes, with the bases as heads and the capitals in the form of rattles, a clear evocation of *Kukulkán*, the plumed serpent. In front of the portico rises a majestic statue of *Chac Mool*, a personage in reclining position who bears a vessel for offerings on the chest. It is believed to be a sort of emissary between the gods and men; likewise, according to the degree of reclining, it could be a mark of equinoxes or solstices. The interior of the temple includes two enclosures whose three vaulted roofs were held up by 12 pilasters sculpted with warriors on all four sides.

The walls have low benches and the wall at the end displays a large altar decorated with reliefs of plumed serpents and held up by 19 small atlases. The walls used to be decorated with scenes of daily life, battles and human sacrifices. The outside walls are decorated with large masks of the god of rain and panels of plumed serpents from whose jaws a man emerges.

Temples of the Tables and of the Chac Mool

The Temple of the Tables rises to the north of the Temple of the Warriors and closes the central plaza on the northeastern side. It is a pyramidal structure in four sections. The upper temple has an access portico and two bays; the jambs and the columns are decorated with reliefs and the back part has an altar supported by small atlases. During the exploration work part of a frieze was recovered decorated with rampant jaguars among vegetation, plumed serpents and groups of darts. It has a substructure with jambs decorated with polychrome reliefs of warriors.

Inside the Temple of the Warriors a substructure known as the "Temple of the Chac Mool" was discovered, a building very similar to that of the Warriors, but of smaller dimensions. It is a base with three stepped sections, finished off by a temple with two bays whose covering is held up by eight pilasters; in front of the access portico there is a sculpture of a *Chac Mool*. The building is noteworthy for the excellent murals decorating the walls, with scenes of lords seated on cushions and jaguar thrones wearing masks of gods; some present offerings, others have shields and scepters and some others carry *átlatl* or dart throwers, darts or small lances.

▼ Detail of one of the small atlases holding up the altar of the Temple of the Warriors, symbolizing those who hold up the sky.

▼ Serpent's head that finishes the beams of the staircase of the Temple of the Warriors. Over it the sculpture of a standard-bearer stands out.

The Steam Bath

It was built to the southeast of the great colonnade, just south of a ball court as yet unexplored. It is a long building with a four-column access portico; a small door leads to the back chamber where the stones were heated and cold water was poured over them to produce the steam. The room had drainage and openings in the roof to let the vapor out. The steam bath had therapeutic and medicinal qualities; it is related to purification rituals and also to the ball game.

The Market

It is located south of the Group of the Thousand Columns and is a complex with access portico and square interior patio flanked by narrow columns and galleries. Both the columns and footways have

reliefs; next to the access is an altar decorated with human figures and serpents. In fact it is not a market but an enclosure reserved for warrior lineages or clans.

Group of the Thousand Columns

The Thousand Columns were a magnificent enclosure of 22,500 m^2, roofed by vaults held up by columns and it was apparently used as a great gallery for warriors or nobles. On the columns 2,211 men walking are represented which mark a processional route moving towards the steps of the Temple of the Warriors. They are bearing dart throwers, small lances and bundles of darts, clubs or axes. Some of the warriors appear to be veterans and show amputations. It is highly notable that each one has its own portrait and their physiognomy differs with regard to the others. Other personages are perhaps wizards or priests and carry offerings. The columns standing in front of the stairs of the Temple of Chac Mool show tied-up prisoners who allude to the celebration of victory.

◀ Relief of one of the warriors that decorate the structure of the Thousand Columns. Each one is different from the others; they may be portraits of historical personages. As a whole, they signal a procession passing through the enclosure.

▸ Chichanchob or "Red House"

This is a sober building with two bays that rises on a base with a single section; it has two crestings, the central one with fretwork and the front one with large masks of *Chaac*. In the front room we can see a red band (hence its name). It has inscriptions with the dates September 15, 869 and June 16, 870, and three personages are mentioned, *Yax-Uk-Kawil*, *Kakupakal* and *Kul Cocom*, who practice rituals of blood spilling and creation of fire. In the back part of the building a ball game was designed and built during the Maya-Toltec period.

▾ The Ossuary or Tomb of the Great Priest

This is a walled precinct with three platforms, a base and a *sacbé* leading to the group of the Xtoloc cenote. The "Platform of the Tombs" supports six votive columns, houses two tombs and has a frieze showing serpents. The second platform is very similar to that of Venus, with the same designs but smaller. The Third Platform is round. "The Ossuary" or "Tomb of the Great Priest" is a replica on a smaller scale of the Castle; it is a pyramid in seven sections with four stairways and beams decorated with serpents. The upper sections had reliefs of birds, fruits, seeds and jewels. The upper temple had a portico of serpent-shaped columns; the frieze was decorated with reliefs of the serpent-bird man, personages with masks and large masks of the god of rain. In the interior of the temple a pas-

sageway was built leading to an extended cave under the building. The only stela on the site was found in this group and it mentions *Kakupakal* or "Smoking shield" and is dated 894 A.D.

▼ House of the Deer

It closes off the plaza on the northeastern side and is a *Puuc* building with characteristics similar to those of Chichanchob, with a façade of plain walls and frieze, simple molding and remains of cresting. Its name is due to the fact that it had a painting of a deer, which has now been lost.

The Observatory or Caracol

To the east of the Chichanchob rises the famous building of the Observatory or Caracol, which consists of a large rectangular platform in a single section with a discreet slope, rounded corners and cornices that delimit an upper plain frieze. It measures 67 m from north to south and 52 m from east to west; at the front it has a broad staircase delimited by beams decorated with intertwined serpents.

The base supports a second square section of 24 m per side which at the same time serves as the base for a round building. The structure was constructed in four stages and its building was ordered between the years 900 and 1000 A.D. The second level was designed first as a circular platform 11 m in diameter which was later expanded to 16 m; in a third stage a rectangular platform was added with a staircase at the front and it finally acquired its definitive form.

The edifice of the Observatory is a cylindrical tower that had three sections and was finished off with a wide cornice; the façade is decorated with large masks of the god of rain and sculptures of seated personages on the accesses. It has a double interior wall that forms two circular concentric chambers, roofed in a masterly manner with vaults and access is through four doors facing the cardinal points. In the central chamber there is a solid nucleus which houses an interior spiral staircase, which gives the building its name and permits access to the upper level.

In appearance, the tower in its first stage had only the central mass and the staircase. The third space is largely destroyed, but conserves a series of windows oriented in different directions which were perhaps used to make astronomic observations. The total height of the tower is 13 m, but it reaches 22.5 m if the base is added.

Complex of the Nuns

This is the largest architectural complex of the classic epoch of Chichén Itzá and apparently the site's guiding center during that period. Owing to the number of rooms it has, in the 16th century Fray Diego de Landa compared it to a convent and that is why it received that name. The building stands out for the amalgam of features in the *Puuc, Chenes* and *Maya-Toltec* styles and was the result of a number of diverse modifications and alterations, as shown by the seven building stages or superimpositions that have been detected. It has three main structures: The Nuns, the East Annex and the Southeast Annex. The Nuns is a massive rectangular base in one single section 10 m high, rounded corners, molded skirting, upper frieze decorated with large masks of *Chaac* and broad staircase limited by beams to the north. The original base, which was of smaller dimensions, underwent three extensions, in the last of which part of the East Annex was covered. From the base rises a rectangular building with eight bays and twelve accesses. The main northern façade is decorated with beautiful panels of stepped frets, lattices, small columns and squares, whereas the rest have frets, tied small columns and lozenges with rosettes. It seems that the construction had cresting, but it was done away with to raise a small temple decorated with small columns and its stairway. The lintels have inscriptions with very interesting texts, as they are bilingual, that is, they are written in the learned Cholana tongue of inscriptions, but also include the translation into Yucatecan Maya.

The Church

The Church received this name for its closeness to the Nuns and is one of Chichén Itzá's most beautiful structures, both for its rich ornamentation and for its balanced proportions. It was built between 800 and 900 A.D. in the *Puuc* style, with a single vaulted bay and access to the west; the walls of the façade are plain in the lower part, whereas the upper part is profusely decorated with stone mosaics: over the level of the access there is a band decorated with stepped frets; behind we can see a broad frieze decorated with large, elabo-

rate masks of *Chaac*, the long-nosed rain god, which alternate with niches that represent personages identified as the four *bacabs*. These, the deities of the four cardinal directions, were in charge of holding up the sky, and are represented by the armadillo, the snail, the turtle and the crab. The upper cornice is decorated with a strip of toothed elements which could represent a very stylized undulating serpent. The building is finished off by a high cresting which includes masks of *Chaac* and stepped frets.

Eastern Annex of the Nuns

The Eastern Annex of the Nuns is a long building with a rectangular base which houses three parallel galleries with a total of eight rooms. The architectural style of this construction is *Chenes*, which is contemporary with the *Puuc* style (Late Classic period, 800-1000 A.C.). The north and south façades are magnificently decorated based on lattice-work and two masks of the god of rain superimposed at the corners. The frieze is framed by moldings and was also

▲ Detail of the personage who stands out in the center of the façade of the Annex of the Nuns. It is a *Kujul Ajaw* or Divine Lord on a celestial throne or even a representation of the lord *Kakupakal* in his personification of the sun. The feathers framing him symbolize the nature of the paradise where he is.

decorated with large masks of *Chaac* at the corners and over the doors, interpolated with lattice-work panels; the upper molding has zigzagging toothed elements that could represent a stylized serpent. The main façade, the eastern one, stands out for the fusion of styles, for it is decorated like a zoomorphic façade typical of the *Chenes* style, although with many masks of *Chaac* in the *Puuc* style. The upper part of the access shows a series of hooks representing the fangs of the earth monster, an evocation of the Maya underworld; a small platform at the foot of the door was also decorated with fangs to symbolize the great jaw. However, in the upper part where the eyes of the reptile should go, there are a number of large masks. In the center of the façade, over the access, appears a large feather arch.

Southeastern Annex of the Nuns

The Southeastern Annex corresponds to the Itzá period and therefore to the *Maya-Toltec* style; it is a small patio flanked by structures of columns that supported wooden beams and lintels.

▶ Detail of one of the reliefs decorating the Temple of the Carved Panels. The central motif is a fertility and life ceremony presided by warriors.

Temple of the Carved Panels

This building of the Maya-Toltec stage closes off the plaza of The Nuns on the eastern side. It is the result of two construction phases: in the first a low base was built with a staircase to the west, finished off by a temple with a portico of two serpentine columns and a back room with an altar at the far end; in the second the staircase was eliminated to add a building with a four-column portico and ample interior enclosure with a double row of columns that supported the roof; the walls are flanked by footways. A new staircase was built in front of the façade to access the original temple on the roof of the new building.

The structure receives its name from the sculpted panels that decorate the walls of the northern and southern façades of the second epoch, with beautiful reliefs showing scenes of warriors presiding over a fertility ceremony among birds, serpents, monkeys, jaguars, trees, plants, flowers and a hut.

▲ The Akab Dzib

The name means "dark writing," by virtue of the inscriptions on one of its lintels. It is an enormous and sober building of the early *Puuc* stage located east of The Nuns. It has a long ground plan with the main façade facing east, decorated with a plain frieze delimited by a molding of three elements. The building houses three sections with 18 vaulted chambers and six accesses. The lintel shows a ruler seated on a throne with an inscription. This is apparently related to the *Yahaual Cho* lineage, "The divine *Cocom*," and the dates 869, 870 and, in particular, 880 A.D. can be read (11 *tun* 1 *ajaw*), which might perhaps be the date of inauguration

Old Chichén or The Group of the Initial Series

This complex, also known as Group of the Phalluses, "Group of the Date" or "Old Chichén," is 800 m to the south of the complex of The Nuns, which is joined to it by a *sacbé*. It is raised on a walled platform and is made up of eight main buildings, three platforms and some housing complexes; it has six accesses, the main one in the form of a great arch with a Maya vault and rounded walls.

Among the main structures the "Platform of the Turtle" stands out, a round structure with two staircases that takes on the form of a great turtle, a land and water element related to the creation myth and the Orion constellation.

Also notable is the "Temple of the Initial Series," which is the only

pyramid-shaped construction in the group and consists of three sloping sections with a staircase to the west and an upper temple; this building, which dates from 600 A.D., was constructed in four stages: the "Structure of the Stuccos" corresponds to the first, a modest three-room residential construction, of which only the foundations remain; the "Temple of the Sacrifices" is a single-section square base with a staircase with struts; prominent in the portico of the upper temple is a sacrificial stone; the "Temple of the Atlas Columns" crowned a three-section sloping base with a *Chac Mool* in front of the stairs; this structure was dismantled and only the columns carved as atlases remain; the final stage corresponds to the "Temple of the Initial Series," a small square building constructed with the materials of the preceding stage. It is possible that the lintels held up by the atlases came from the Building of the Phalluses and is well-known for being the only one on the site that possesses a complete initial series with the date 10.2.9.1.9, 9 *Muluk 7 Zak*, which corresponds to July 30, 878 A.D. It also mentions the lords *Kakupakal* and *Kinil Kupol*.

The largest complex in the group is the "Palace of the Phalluses," which is made up of various enclosures; the most famous is the so-called "House of the Phalluses," which has eleven vaulted rooms and a second level decorated in the *Puuc* and *Maya-Tolteca* styles; it receives its name from the sculptures that decorate the bays. The decoration of the façade includes lattices and 16 panels adorned with scenes of *pawahtunes* (deities of the wind) performing rites of penis perforation and bleeding. The southern and northern extremes open out onto two small columned patios and in one there is a small staircase leading to the upper temple. The "House of Snails" receives its name from the sculptures that decorate the molding of the frieze, elements linked to life, rebirth and the underworld.

"The House of the Atlas Columns" owes its name to the sculptures of the portico. "The Temple of the Owls is called thus because of the sculptures that decorate the pillars and the jambs; on the frieze there are owls with their wings spread which alternate with human figures bearing long picks and instruments of self-sacrifice. The moldings have sculptures of turtles and the corners large masks of *Chaac*. The "Gallery of the Monkeys" has friezes decorated with amusing figures of monkeys interacting with men dressed up as birds.

Balamkanché Caves

The name means "altar or throne of the wizard or of the jaguar". They are 5 km to the east of the site and are a system of caves 800 m long with numerous galleries and a cenote. In various chambers the Maya deposited many offerings of braziers, effigies, incense burners, vessels and stone metates dedicated to the god of rain.

Discover *Mexico* in full color

Our guides will help you get to know all about Mexico's archaeological, historical, artistic and cultural wealth.

Did you know that the Maya established trade routes, that their gods were symbolized in the shape of animals and that they created two calendars, a solar one and a ritual one**?**

You will find all this information and much more in the different titles we have available in several languages